Breaking Chains
30 Days to Freedom From Your Marijuana Habit

Welcome! Glad you are reading this. I hope you will find this guide to be useful and inspiring. It is just that— a guide. I do not intend to tell you how to live or preach that what I have learned is the only truth. I just want to share some things I have learned in hopes that they will be helpful for others with similar experiences.

If you want to get the most out of this, I suggest that you **do** the exercises. They are not that hard. The act of writing is very therapeutic and clarifying. You will benefit. The morning page exercise is not an original idea of mine. It is a therapeutic exercise with support from a variety of fields. Try it out.

The exercise plan is just a guideline also. Do what works for you based on your level of physical fitness. The goal is not to train until you are miserable, the goal is to get some blood pumping and burn off some mental energy in a physical way. If you have a fitness program that works for you, stick to that. The point is just to do something and to do it consistently.

For the purposes of this course, I am assuming that you currently have a psychological dependency on marijuana. Some people use marijuana and do not develop a psychological dependency. This guide is not an intention to convert or judge anyone. It is intended to help people who **do** have a marijuana dependency learn skills to overcome that dependency.

As you break psychological ties there are often physical symptoms. These are usually worse in the earliest days. None of the physical symptoms of marijuana withdrawal should be life threatening. If you use marijuana in a medically prescribed manner, talk to your physician before starting this program or any program like it.

I am not a doctor. I am not a psychologist. I am not an expert. I am a regular person who used to smoke too much pot and found freedom from that habit. I can't guarantee this program because I can't make you quit anything. Your husband, wife, friends, parents, preacher, therapist or state court can't make you quit. If you have a dependency on marijuana, you will use until **YOU** decide not to.

You will have to make that decision to abstain every day. Some days will be harder than others. Power through. A single use, one puff of a joint, will wreck the whole thing. It will send you right back to where you started or worse. If you do fail, pick yourself up and move forward. It is not the end of the world.

Make it a point not to fail. A major component of this whole process is keeping promises to yourself. When you make a decision that you are abstaining from marijuana, honor that decision. It will be hard, but you will gain respect for yourself. That self respect will pour over into other aspects of your life and you will become stronger.

You can do it.

Ready for the five word phrase that will make your life/quit journey much more manageable?

"I am taking a break."

You don't have to convince yourself that you are quitting forever. Commit to thirty days. At the end of thirty days you can reevaluate if you like. Don't reevaluate before the end. Commit to thirty days. When thirty days seems overwhelming, commit to the present day. "I will not use marijuana today."

When we use the Q word (quit) the dependent portion of our brain cringes and goes crazy. When we call it a break, it takes the pressure off. It is not so scary.

When your friends bug you to come get high, you don't have to try to explain that you 'quit.' You can say you are taking a break and they are more likely to leave you alone.

I am willing to bet that after thirty days you will enjoy your newfound freedom so much that you have no interest in returning to your old habits.

A Few Notes

You will be more likely to succeed if you begin this program without any marijuana in your possession. Some people have success with throwing away their stash, other people establish a quit date and taper off usage until then/until they run out. Some people are able to maintain the willpower to stop using while they still have a stash. Breaking your habit while you are in possession will be the hardest method. Any extra steps that you can put between yourself and marijuana use will be helpful, especially in the first days.

Picking a day to run out by is also not the best. When you do this it is easy to fall into a loop of "one last time." I have smoked quite a few "last" joints and bowls. This way of thinking can be harmful to both your momentum and your faith in your ability to keep promises to yourself. You will need both of those things in the next 30 days. The best course of action is to get rid of your stash. Not by smoking it all in one "last" mad dash, but by actually getting rid of it. Throw it away if you can or give it away if you feel you need to. This will probably cause you to feel feelings of attachment and then loss. We will talk more about that in the coming days. Realize that those feelings are a symptom of dependency. Use your rational mind and realize that
Throwing away a little bit of pot is not the end of the world.
You can always get some more.

Throwing away your stash can serve as a symbol for the beginning of the journey you are about to start. You do not have to get rid of your paraphernalia yet if you don't want to. Remember you are "taking a break." We will deal with paraphernalia later, but for now lock it up somewhere, put it under your bed or in your attic. Out of sight, out of mind.

The first 2-5 days will be the hardest physically and mentally. Once you power through those you will find it easier to progress. You have already shown the initiative to break your habit, now you need to protect that initiative. If it is at all possible, avoid situations where marijuana is present for at least the first few days. I realize that this is not always possible due to work/living situations, but really try to see if you can swing something. If you smoke at work every day, see if you can get a couple days off. If your roommates smoke, see if you can get out of town or stay with family for a couple days. I understand that this is not always possible. You can overcome any situation, but you will be battling with your brain for a little while and any way you can stack the odds in your favor will help.

I have listed some dietary supplements that you may find useful. The first few days, anything you can do to make yourself comfortable will be helpful. Your brain is going to miss its THC. By rewarding yourself in healthy ways, you will speed along the rewiring process.

I also suggest going to the bookstore or library and picking up a few books that interest you. Keep your mind occupied in a productive manner. Download a few movies or TV series for when you need to just turn your brain off, but it is also beneficial to provide some stimulation.

Some people experience insomnia as they withdraw from marijuana. Some of the listed supplements help with that. Getting lots of sunshine and exercise during the day will also help you to sleep better. Tire yourself out and sleep will be your reward.

Part of successfully breaking a marijuana habit is making yourself as comfortable as possible and part of it is just dealing with/powering through the uncomfortable parts. The worst of it is over quickly. Power through! Keep going one day a time, even one minute at a time when you need to.

If you don't think you can break your marijuana dependency, rest assured that you can. I know because I didn't think I could break mine, and I did. I do not have any sort of superhuman willpower. Once you set your mind on freedom, all you have to do is put the work in and keep moving in that direction. I hope you will find this guide helpful.

Feel free to read this book start to finish in one or a few sittings. It will work most effectively with your quit journey if you read each day's passage on that particular day as well. You will maybe read something that is applicable to you that day. More importantly, you are bringing your **decision** to refrain from marijuana use back into the front of your mind. Daily reading and thinking are action steps that will help you achieve that.

Best,
Nick

www.expothead.com

Exercise Plan

Plan to exercise.

That is one of several dumb jokes hidden throughout this guide. If you find them all, you don't get a prize.

Seriously though, this plan is not about exercise. Exercise and physical activity are an important component, but I am leaving what that looks like up to you. There are lots of great, free resources online. Most gyms will give you a free trial period of a week or a month. Bodyweight exercises like situps, pushups and pull-ups are free and effective. Cardio is helpful.
Try to alternate short/intense cardio with long/easy cardio. Just going for a walk is good for your mind and body and is a nice way to ease into more strenuous exercise.

Combine fun and exercise when you can. Playing soccer, tennis or basketball are great. Ride a bike or rollerblade. Swimming, yoga, you get the idea. Just try to get yourself moving for a half hour or so most days of the week. You can use a quick set of 10 or so pushups or squats as a way to take your mind off of cravings when they occur.

THC is stored in fat. When you stop smoking, it sticks around for a while. The more fat you burn, the more you sweat, the faster you will feel better physically. Sweat if you can, especially during the first few days of detox.

Helpful Supplements

There are a few supplements/creature comforts that will make your break, especially the first few days, easier.

Dark chocolate- eat a piece for cravings/reward. Try to eat it slow and really savor it.

Sunflower seeds/chewing gum- Same idea. They also provide something to do with your hands and mouth, which helps with some of the associative part of breaking the addiction.

Melatonin- Can help if you are having trouble getting to sleep.

Chamomile tea- A cup before bed can also help get to sleep. I like the Celestial Seasonings Sleepytime Blend.

Vitamin D- Improves mood. Best to get it via sunshine but if your location/season don't permit you can get it in pill form.

Niacin- Thought to help fight depression. Also helps to burn fat, getting you through Detox quicker.

Epsom Salt- A good source of Magnesium. An Epsom Salt bath is a good reward, and the soak feels great on tired muscles. If you don't have a bathtub, put some in a bucket with hot water and soak your feet.

Try to eat lots of veggies and avoid processed sugars. Your brain is going to be a little unhappy that its THC source has been cut off and it will take that out on your body. Eating well, exercise and little rewards will help that process to go by smoother and more quickly.

*A Note on Alcohol Use

I recommend trying to avoid alcohol during these next 30 days. That said, I did drink a few beers during my first week or two off of marijuana. I can't tell you what to do, but be aware that alcohol loosens your convictions and lowers your inhibitions starting pretty much with the first sip. It is hard on your body and generally unkind to your mind. I have noticed that most people who use marijuana as their drug of choice are not drawn as strongly to alcohol, but you should still exercise caution. It is unproductive to swap one addiction for another, and an alcohol addiction can have much more harmful effects than a marijuana habit. Shoot for total sobriety and clarity if you can.

DAY ONE

"The journey of a thousand miles begins with a single step." - Lao Tzu

Congratulations. You have shown initiative and have done what is often the hardest act- you have **decided** to make a change. Today is day one. Together we will be embarking on a 30 day journey to free ourselves of negative patterns and habits, to find where some of these patterns came from, and to internalize new, positive, habits and practices.

For some people, the first day of abstaining from marijuana is relatively easy, and for some people it is excruciating. If you are in either camp, rest easy, we are running a marathon and not a sprint. We will take each day individually while also keeping an eye on the big picture.

If you are a habitual smoker, you still have plenty of THC in your system today. Your brain has not yet even really noticed that its supplies are dwindling and therefore has not yet reacted in force.

Any withdrawal symptoms today are mainly psychological. When a person goes without food, the body can live off fat reserves for weeks. The hunger pains of the first day or hours, while intense, are mainly psychological. This applies to you as well.

Today, your goal is to be easy and good to yourself. Take advantage of the momentum you have found. Feelings of guilt and loss can cause anxiety and stress and will be counterproductive. Be kind to yourself internally. Manifest this externally by treating yourself.

Take yourself out to lunch or dinner, or pick up a nice meal at the grocery store and cook it. Take yourself out for ice cream or a chocolate bar. Indulge yourself. Tell yourself- I am doing a good and hard thing and I deserve to reward myself. Previously, our reward system was marijuana. Getting high was the ultimate reward for any hard or tiring task. The world is beautiful and good, and there are many other ways to find reward. Our goal today is to remember that.

There is a task associated with treating yourself: mindfulness. When you eat your juicy steak or rich ice cream, eat it slowly and savor the flavors. Enjoy the texture, the presentation, the smell. Take pleasure in the full feeling in your stomach. If weather permits, take a walk when you are done eating. Appreciate the air, the trees, your body.

Take a hot shower or bath, drink some chamomile tea and/or take a melatonin, and drift off to sleep. Before you get in bed, remind yourself again that you are doing a good thing. You are on the path towards freedom of the mind. As you are getting in bed, think "I am so tired. I have never been so tired before. I can't wait until my head hits the pillow and I can find peace in sleep."

If you have eaten well, and gotten some fresh air exercise, you should have not too much trouble falling asleep. The tea and melatonin and mental exercise of convincing yourself you are tired should help tip things over the edge. When you wake up, you will have already arrived at.....

DAY TWO

DROP AND GIVE ME TEN!

Dead serious. Stop what you're doing right now and do ten pushups and ten jumping jacks. If you are not in ten pushup shape, do them leaning against a counter or table.

Alright, got the blood flowing. Feels pretty good, huh? You're in for a tough one today. Day two can be one of the hardest days in the whole process. But **you** are a hard individual. You just did exercise at the drop of a hat. And more than physical exercise, you exercised agency.

Agency? The idea that **you** are the captain of your ship. You cannot control the world but you can control your reaction to the world. Sometimes that is why we used- an effort to control one portion of our reality. This strategy winds up backfiring and eventually marijuana begins to control many aspects of our reality. No mas. You are on day **two** of fully seizing control of your own mind and life.

You made it through the first day. Let's get through the second day. Your only task today is to not smoke any pot. The second day is a powerful psychological barrier. In your mind you may chalk the first day up to a fluke, or a supreme and short lived exercise in willpower. Once you get through two days, you recognize that you have the **power** to abstain. Momentum is building. More THC is leaving your body.

You may feel physically worse today. Headaches, nausea, insomnia are all possible and maybe even probable. Deal with them now or they will haunt you forever. You won't die. You will maybe be a little bit uncomfortable. Have you ever seen someone detox from opiates or alcoholism? They are sweating and puking and shaking and crying. Be thankful that is not your reality today. Take an aspirin, take a walk, take a benadryl. Pour yourself an ice cold coca cola or a warm glass of milk and sit in the sun or by the fire.

You are fighting a hard battle. Remember yesterday's advice to be good to yourself. Eat your favorite food for dinner, watch a funny movie, go sit someplace pretty and watch the sunset. Today there is more to focus on than just being good to yourself-

Steel yourself.

If you were going to fight a boxing match, you would make sure you were well fed and well rested. You would also be visualizing victory, singlemindedly focused on it, almost pissed off about it. That is how you approach day two. Take care of the easy variables of comfort, and then set your mind to the purpose at hand: freedom from marijuana.

> Exercise.
> Breathe.
> Write this affirmation 15 times- **"I am breaking myself free from the chains of marijuana."**

DAY 3

Congratulations.

Two days in. You are getting the hang of it. Yesterday you no doubt fought through some cravings. There were times you thought about getting high and instead you abstained. This is tremendous mental progress.

Seriously, tremendous.

As a habitual smoker, you have created patterns of use. You are triggered, you fantasize, you obsess, you obtain pot and you get high. Over and over again. Yesterday, you were triggered, and you shut it down. Today you're going to do it again. Each time you abstain from an impulse to use your brain says, "whoa man."

Your brain is like a dog. The dog barks. It keeps barking. If you ignore it, it will eventually stop. If you give it a treat to shut it up, guess what it just learned?

Impulses to use are the barking. Marijuana is the treat. Now you are abstaining/ignoring and you are learning how to be a good dog (brain) parent. The great thing about the human brain is that it is flexible. Human beings can learn to adapt to almost anything. It will not be long until your brain has rewired itself to seek reward in other ways, and to quickly shut down impulses to use.

You will maybe have lots of energy today. You may feel a natural high. If not today, expect it tomorrow. Every person's mind and body are different but it is a consistent experience among people who stop using to feel a burst of energy and awareness around day 2-5. We are going to put this little burst to work.

Here is your task. Sit down, preferably first thing in the morning, take a pen and paper (no computers) and write for three pages. You can write whatever you want. Don't think too much, don't stop to edit. Just dump your brain out on paper. If you get stuck start describing the room you are in, what you had for breakfast, your deepest darkest fears and insecurities. Seriously though, write three pages. Once you start it will flow. This is a therapeutic exercise. Feel free to talk about your feelings since abstaining, your thoughts on your past use, your goals. Nothing is too big or small to write about. The purpose of this exercise is to skim a little bit of the noise off the top of your head. You are going through a psychologically strenuous time and it will make you feel better and lighter and clearer to put some of those whirling thoughts to rest on paper.

You are starting to experience momentum in a positive way. You have always experienced momentum. It is an inescapable force and a universal scientific law. But now you have seized **control** of it and started to steer it the other way. Your old momentum was to smoke and keep smoking. To break commitments to yourself and others and keep breaking them. To sleep in today and then sleep in tomorrow too.

Now you have started doing the **work** of rerouting that momentum. I am proud of you and you should be proud of yourself.

Remember exercise today also. Protect your momentum. Refuse to fail.

DAY 4

Did you dream last night?

Getting my dreams back was one of my favorite parts of life without weed. Last night I dreamed that I was in the Alps chasing down mountain goats. I've smoked some pretty funky stuff in my time, but I always knew what continent I was on.

If you are looking for a mind altering experience, your own healthy, sleeping brain is hard to beat.

Fun and games aside, there is a lot of important subconscious work that goes on while we dream. Dreams serve as sort of a bridge between the conscious and the subconscious, reality and imagination. I don't know the science behind it, but my belief is that marijuana works on some of those same waves, and that is why normal dreaming behavior is absent in most heavy smokers.

Cultures across the globe and throughout history have placed great importance on dreams, seeing them as gateways to both our own selves and spiritual realms we cannot see.

Dreams are sacred. They are hard to explain, but as we study them we can learn from them things that we don't see with the waking mind. This is a more pure and fruitful experience than the ones we would try to self-induce with marijuana. We have to be patient with our minds. When we try to tap into these subconscious waves over and over at our own leisure, we dilute the power. You know this. The beautiful and revelatory highs from when you started smoking have been gone for a while now. They were an illusion anyway.

Now you are gaining back the control of your mind, and it is thanking you by giving you the gift of dreams.

Cherish your new dreams for this reason also. They are one of the first tangible things you notice yourself getting back as you begin to break free from marijuana. Rest assured that many more wonderful things will return to you, and you will even be given **new** wonderful things that you did not know existed.

Your ambition, your focus, your joy; all these things **will** come back to you in time just as sure as your dreams came back to you in a short period of time.

Today, write your three pages again. Try to do it first thing in the morning, and if you had dreams, try to include them in your writing.

Doing this cements them, and will make tomorrow's dreams easier to remember. Be on the lookout for messages in your dreams. Your subconscious has missed you and it may have a lot to tell you.

Many people say that the first 72 hours of quitting marijuana are the hardest physically. Congratulations, you are past that. You are hopefully feeling strong and empowered. Continue to be kind to yourself and reaffirm yourself. Today, write this affirmation 15-20 times:

"I am proud of myself for the work I am doing to break free of marijuana. I am excited to continue on this path."

Day 5

We have arrived at day 5, the Friday of your first week at the pot quitting office. Feel free to wear jeans and a Hawaiian shirt today.

You should be proud of what you are accomplishing. You are building good momentum and should be pretty much past the worst of the physical cravings. But don't let up, certain parts of your brain will still try to sabotage you.

Now that you are five days in, we are going to take the gloves off a little and look at some things that might feel a little unpleasant. You can handle it.

As recovering addicts, we need to realize certain things. We need to be honest with ourselves that the feelings we used to chase were not based in reality. They were illusions. As you get further away, your brain will have a tendency to remember only the positive things. This is called positivity bias. We are naturally inclined to remember the good parts and forget the bad parts.

For a recovering addict (or anyone), this is dangerous and needs to be shut down quickly. Your brain will say "Hey remember how much fun we used to have smoking weed? Remember how good it felt?"

Here you have a choice. You can say "wow Brain, you're right. Getting high was the best... let me fantasize about it and then walk myself right into obsession and then on into actual use."
Or
You can say, "Back the f*#& up Brain. What about all the time I spent feeling groggy? What about driving all the way across town to pick up a sack? What about all the bad feelings?

You can choose to live and deal in illusion, or you can choose to live and deal in reality. Sometimes reality is unpleasant. That is not a good excuse to avoid it. As we learn to deal with and eventually embrace reality, we learn how to direct and shape our reality. Gaining freedom from substance abuse is the first step. No matter how productive or functional we were as users, we still had an escape hatch on reality. When things got too hard or too weird, we shut down and sparked up. On a long timeline, this leads to stunting of personal growth and loss of healthy coping skills.

As a full and healthy human being, you should and will be able to cope with anything life throws at you without having to retreat to mind altering substances. That is the journey we are on.

Do your pages again today, get some exercise, get some fresh air. Spend a little time today tidying up your work and living space. You probably have an abundance of energy, put it to work and use the momentum to build productive habits.

Today's affirmation-

"I am free to exist in reality."

Day 6

Today you get a break from writing your three pages. If you feel inclined, feel free to, but today's homework is a little different. Right now, write down five things you are grateful for. They can be abstract or tangible, big or small. Write them as full sentences- "I am grateful for my parents." "I am grateful for the sun on my face."

Gratitude is a powerful thing. Many times feeling sorry for ourselves and the desire to use go hand in hand. When we feel and live gratitude, we are not feeling sorry for ourselves. It is a matter of framing. When we are coming from a place of gratitude, we are also coming from a place of peace and acceptance. We are ok with our lot in life, and more than that we feel fortunate and blessed.
Right now your brain may be trying to fight you. You maybe lost some of the feeling of excitement about not smoking. Part of you wishes you could just ditch all this self improvement and go get high. You are maybe grumbling internally, "this sucks, this is dumb, my life wasn't so bad and now I'm all stressed out and irritable and I just want to smoke and I caaaaan't."

If you stay there, you risk getting trapped in a negative feedback loop. We are only so strong. After a while of this complaining and questioning we will say, "screw it, roll one." Don't do that. Choose instead to shut down the negative feedback loop. This is achieved through, you guessed it, gratitude. When you catch yourself starting to grumble, go back to gratitude. Be grateful for your health, for your life, for your mind. We live in a culture that is obsessed with comparison. How can I be grateful for my Ford Explorer when my neighbor has a Hummer??

There are people **RIGHT NOW** who will **DIE** today because **THEY DON'T HAVE ANY FOOD.**
How can we complain about anything? We are blessed beyond measure.

Gratitude goes the other way. It is incompatible with comparison and complaining. Gratitude says- "I am so thankful that I have a vehicle, and legs to press the pedals, and eyes to see the road, and that I live in a country that provides roads." Gratitude says-

"I am grateful that I am experiencing stress. It feels good to feel. I am grateful that I am no longer numbing my mind. I am grateful that this irritation will pass quickly. I am grateful that I have the agency and the willpower to break free from addiction. I am grateful for the opportunity to adjust my thought patterns, habits and behavior. **I will continue on this path of growth."**

Gratitude turns into momentum. When we tell ourselves that we are grateful, we become grateful. When we become grateful, we feel responsible for expressing our gratitude. We can express our gratitude by living well and making the most of our opportunities. We remember and recognize that when we used to be stoned, we were not making the most of our opportunities. We decide to move forward on the path to freedom.

Choose your own affirmation today. Focus on something you are grateful for. Let yourself be overwhelmed by the feeling. Feel the healing that takes place when we focus on what we have instead of what we do not have.

DAY 7
One week! Nice work. One week ago, you were on day one. Now you have made it through the cycle of one whole week. You should be proud of yourself. It is maybe getting easier. Hopefully you are learning new things about yourself and feeling growth. It is good to

stop and feel the sense of accomplishment. Think about a few months ago- you would have never thought you could or would go a week without smoking pot.

This can be a tricky week. Expect bad feelings. You are not out of the woods yet, and your brain will continue to push back against your new progress. You may have feelings of despair, despondency and rage. It is important to push through these. They are temporary. If you defeat them now, they will go away. Here is an example-

I used to love to get high and play guitar. Felt great, I was in tune with the music, my body felt nice, I was in the zone. After a week or so off weed I tried to play guitar- my fingers felt stuck, my mind was blurry, I was not happy. I felt "this is stupid, this sucks, now I can't even enjoy the things I used to." I thought maybe I would never be able to enjoy playing music again without being stoned. How many other things would I no longer be able to enjoy? What was the point?

These are toxic feelings and they don't come from a place of truth. Your mind is still rebalancing itself. If you start to do an activity that you formerly associated with using marijuana and find you do not enjoy it, just put it down for a bit. Recognize that your mind is going through some pretty serious psychological changes. Your brain is not unhappy about playing guitar, your brain is unhappy that it is expecting to get a dose of THC and you are not giving it that. Think about if you had a cup with a lid on it. You think that there is orange juice in it. You can't wait to take a big long sip of ice cold OJ. You pull on the straw and get a mouthful of milk. Blegh. Even if you like milk, you will be disappointed. You will be disappointed because your expectation did not match the reality. This is what is going on in your brain. You expect a chemical dose and you do not get it. This pisses you off. This is not the milk's fault.

You are at a crucial point. A crisis point even. Will you decide that it is not worth the aggravation to stay clean? Will you let your feelings get the better of you? Look, feelings are great, but they change all the time. If you live based only on feelings, you will never get anywhere.

Will you decide to power through? You have gone seven days, why not go eight? If you give in now, you will continue to be a slave to a substance. You will continue to need to get high before enjoying your favorite activities. If you can go a little longer, trust me, just a few days- it will get better. You will come back to the things you love with renewed vigor and focus. You will play better guitar, make better art, have better relationships. You will learn to manage your mind without external forces.

Do you remember being a kid? Running around or drawing or doing whatever it was you loved to do? Think back to that feeling of joy, when time stopped and all was well in the world. **You were in that place without any marijuana.**

The chemicals and structure for joy and meaning are all inside of you. You don't need to get high to reach that place. When you cultivate a pattern of getting high to reach that place it becomes the only way you can even get close.

You have to walk through some hard places to reach a place of freedom from this.

Keep walking.
Day 8

You have homework this week. You are not allowed to weasel out. It may be uncomfortable, but it will be productive. Here is your homework-

Attend an Alcoholics Anonymous meeting.

"But! I'm not an alcoholic! What if people I know find out?! I can't stand the 12 step crowd! What if they kidnap me and indoctrinate me?!"

You will be ok. You will find that they are friendly and good people who are working through problems and habits that they have. As they share their stories, you will gain perspective and insight into the mind of an addict and will probably be able to draw parallels to your own life. At many meetings I have attended, someone shares a story of relapse. They thought it would be ok to have one drink at a social function or on vacation. A bender inevitably followed. Now they were working through the wreckage. Our substance of choice has many less physical dangers. We are fortunate. But the brain is the same- if we take one toke, we will sabotage all our efforts thus far.

You don't have to speak at the meeting, though you may feel free to. If you do, respect the setting and the people gathered. Alcoholism is a nasty disease. The people who gather together to fight it are strong and courageous and they are your brothers and sisters walking the road to freedom.

Two of our positive keywords this week are **goals** and **habits.**

Our habits move us towards our goals. When we do not have control of our habits, they move us away from our goals and to their own. As we phase out negative habits, we need to fill that space with positive habits. When you have positive habits, you will move towards positive goals.

When we have positive goals, we will naturally fill the blanks in our lives with positive habits. When we were using, it was very hard to have defined goals. My goal most days was to get as high as I could and still maintain a baseline level of functionality. If I did have longer term "goals" they were really more dreams.

 "A goal is a dream with a plan." This is a high school gym coach cliche but it is true.
Marijuana lends itself quite well to daydreaming. It is less effective for planning and taking action.
Remember the old song…

"I was gonna clean my room…. and then I got high."

You have more homework today. Brainstorm your goals. Write them on paper. Write a bunch. Narrow them down to a few concise ideas. Look at them, memorize them, internalize them. Part B of your homework is tomorrow and it will involve your goals list. 5 extra credit points if you can guess which other keyword tomorrow's homework involves.

Remind yourself that these goals are not compatible with your old marijuana habit. That is in the past. Your goals are in the future and you are moving towards them. Your job in the present is to abstain from negative habits (smokin' pot) so that you can move towards progress.

"I am moving towards my true goals and leaving old things in the past."

Day 9

When I was using heavily, I used to think that I was some sort of zen master. I almost never got angry. If someone cut me off in traffic, I thought, "hey maaan, not cool." If someone I was close to wronged me, I thought, "hey maaan, not cool." I honestly believed that I had risen above my anger, that I was some sort of ultra wise stoner sage who had transcended negative feeling.

Boy was I wrong.

It took a few days, but around day 8 or 9 into my quit journey I was **pissed.** About everything. "Look at this asshole over there breathing. Breathing with his lungs and stuff. grumble grumble. " I really was filled with an actual internal rage. It felt like all the anger I had suppressed during my pot smoking career was back and it was bubbling up. I was lashing out at people I love. I was mad at the sky for being blue.

I had forgotten how to feel and deal with anger.

When things don't come out, they fester and get worse. You have likely medicated yourself to a point of numbness. Pot "takes the edge off." In real life, we have to deal with that edge. We have to learn to identify it early and handle it constructively. When you feel this anger and rage, there are a couple practical steps you can take.

Deep breaths are easy, free and very helpful. Take ten when you feel the anger in your stomach. Breathe slow and hard. You can vibrate your lips like a horse when you exhale for extra effect. Feel yourself expelling the rage from inside and let your body loosen.

Exercise. With aggression if possible. Go run back and forth across a field until you want to throw up. Ride your bike as fast as you can. Beat a bag up. You will burn up some of this negative energy and you will feel better.

The good news is that you can actually reframe and redirect this anger in order to help yourself along your journey. Turn that anger on to marijuana. Don't let it turn into anger at yourself, because that can be counterproductive, but be mad at weed. Be mad that it cost you so much time and energy, and that it lied to you. It told you everything would be warm and fuzzy forever, and now here you are experiencing bad feelings because of marijuana.

Use this anger to further entrench yourself into your conviction that **"I do not smoke or want or like or need marijuana anymore."**

These feelings of anger will pass. You are learning to renormalize your emotions. You will learn how to be a little bit angry and to manage that feeling before it gets out of control. You can manage anger without resorting to substance use.

Alright, part two of yesterday's homework. Look at your goal list. Hopefully that was a productive exercise. Spend a few minutes thinking about those goals. Now on another piece of paper, make two columns. One is "Habits I have now" and the other is "Habits I would like to develop to move me towards my goals." Fill 'em up. Habits are the vehicles that move us towards our goals. As we are more aware of our habits, we are able to better steer towards our goals.

Day 10

Welcome to day ten, double digits. It is good to celebrate these milestones. You have made a lot of progress in ten days, and you are well on your way to breaking the grip of a marijuana habit. Keep up the good work.

Today we are going to talk about denial. Denial plays a large part in the addict's mindset and behavior. Denial says

"It's just weed." "It's not addictive." "It's better than drinking." "I don't have a problem." "I can quit whenever I feel like it." "Nobody even notices that I'm stoned."

You have maybe noticed over the past ten days that marijuana had a tighter grip on you than you previously thought. Now that you are starting to get a more objective perspective, you can realize how much it actually was affecting you.

Denial says whatever it wants, whatever you want to hear. Denial is really us telling ourselves "everything is fine, I do not need to put in effort to change."

Denial and marijuana go very well together. Marijuana is sneaky. Other drugs will take you to rock bottom. Marijuana will let you hang out a few steps above rock bottom for years and years. You can set up a comfortable little spot down there and move in. You can convince yourself that your little spot at the bottom of the hole was where you always wanted to end up and then if you have second thoughts about that you can fire up a joint and forget about it. "Oh, was I having a small existential crisis? Now I feel good and I would like some nachos and a nap."

These small existential crises are a normal part of life and they are actually very important in moving us towards where and who we really want to be. Years and years of suppressing these hard conversations with yourself will lead to stunted growth. Denial says-

"my job sucks, pot is the only way I can get through the day there."

A growth mindset realizes that hating a job can and will naturally lead to a desire to move into a better job, and that with focus and good habits that desire can manifest into reality.

In the mind of a person addicted to a substance, that substance is the ultimate reward. Think about when you were using. Imagine you had a nice fat joint rolled up and you were headed outside to smoke it, and then you bumped into an old friend who did not smoke and they struck up a conversation with you. Where would your mind be? Would you fully engaged in the conversation and genuinely happy to see your friend? Or would part of your brain be pretty distracted, and wish they would go away so you could get high in peace?

With marijuana as the ultimate reward, how can you overcome your denial? It doesn't work. Any hard conversation with yourself about what you want is eventually derailed, because what you want is to get high. And that is a pretty easy desire to fulfill. Your brain tricks itself into thinking it is finding fulfillment. All sorts of mental gymnastics occur. The addicted mind can justify almost anything, and it will rarely hold itself accountable.

It is only when we break free from the immediate addiction that we can begin to deal with denial. These things take time. If you are ten days in, you have already dealt a crushing blow to denial. Denial said "You don't have a problem, hit this." And you said **"I do have a problem, but I am working to correct it."** You made the **decision** to recognize and name your marijuana habit and then to stand up against it.

Day 11

One of the uglier aspects of constant marijuana use it the effect it has on our brain's natural reward system. A marijuana habit teaches us that a brief period of contentment is never far away. I think this is where a lot of the stereotype of the 'lazy pothead' comes from. I was not a necessarily a lazy pothead. I had a job and I performed well there. I did side work sometimes and I maintained a pretty decent level of physical fitness. I got through college and I tried to read books and educate myself.

The issue was that if I could not reward myself with marijuana before, during and after these tasks I was a wreck. In order to do something as basic as clean my house, I had to get high before, stop for a bowl in the middle and then when I was done I would reward myself by getting high again. That's not healthy! It's not normal. Maybe your experience was not this extreme or maybe it was. The concept remains the same for habitual users- our ultimate goal and reward at any time is getting our chemical fix of the preferred substance.

Habitual marijuana use conditions us to internalize instant gratification. We come to expect that when things are good, when things are bad, when things are hard, we can normalize and ease the situation with a toke. The brain effect is the same whether you are a heavy or light habitual user. If you are a non casual user, your brain becomes accustomed to a THC rush as a form of reward. If your use consists only of one bowl at the same time every day, this probably does not have much of a net negative effect on your life. But watch your brain- do you not get excited a few minutes before your appointed time? Do you not feel a little out of sorts for some unexplained reason on days when you don't get a chance to use?

At some point in a hard day do you not think, "At least I will be getting stoned later"?

The tricky thing about a marijuana habit is that it is **not** the end of the world. It is a pretty benign drug of choice. You won't make your heart explode and you won't choke on your own vomit. You probably won't rob anybody or prostitute yourself to get a bag of weed. But we are not here to justify, we are here to **improve**. We are here to grow. You obviously have some sort of internal tension regarding your marijuana use or else you wouldn't have dropped the money on this guide or read this far. Don't let the addicted portion of your brain trick you into submission.

Just because marijuana is less harmful than other substances doesn't mean that it is harmless or that habitual use is beneficial. Over the timeline of your entire life, learning to chase and accept instant gratification will lead to all kinds of problems. The best parts of life don't come from easy fixes, they come from **work**. We have to learn to appreciate the work and appreciate the process itself of doing the work.

You are 11 days in to this journey. Every day for the last 11 days you have been rebelling against your desire for instant gratification. You have been doing the work. Hopefully you are seeing results already. If you are not, you will see them soon. You are breaking powerful chemical and psychological ties. That is bound to cause tension and that tension leads to questions. Trust the process. Believe that as you gain ground on your habit that you will see results. If you do as many pushups as you can every day, eventually you will be able to do more pushups. If you run a mile as fast as you can every day, you will eventually be running faster miles. If you continue to abstain from marijuana use **you will eventually see results**.

You are stronger than your habit and you are achieving victory over it every day.

Day 12

Here is the question I want you to think about today: "Why did I spend so much time getting high?"

Really think about it. Think back to when you started and how you went from casual use to frequent use to habitual use. Think about your mindset at each stage along the way. Write it out if that helps. Here is the short version of my answer- I started smoking during a difficult period in my life. I was unsatisfied with a lot of things and when I got high I just felt "**wow** that's nice." I forgot about my dissatisfaction. Pot hit pretty much all my pleasure buttons and I fell right into it. I progressed in my life and career and eventually found satisfaction in a lot of places outside of getting high, but by then it was a habit. It was a crutch I did not want to get rid of, a familiar friend or security blanket. Even as my life got to a place that looked pretty great from the outside, pot was my panic button, my escape hatch. When things got weird or hard or boring, I knew that relief and oblivion was just a few tokes away.

This is just my personal experience, but it seems to be a pretty common thread among habitual and former habitual smokers I have talked with. Habitual users are usually using marijuana to facilitate some sort of **escapism**.

If I had to go to the DMV, you better believe I was going to smoke my brains out beforehand. It almost made it like I wasn't at the DMV. As you normalize this pattern of checking out from situations you don't feel like being in, and as your body requires increasing doses of THC to feel "normal", it becomes much harder to live a fully present life. I was pretty much always either stoned or thinking about getting stoned.

Life is short and beautiful and weird and exciting. It is sad to try and escape from it. What is so bad about real life? Hopefully by this stage in your journey to freedom you are realizing that. When we are habitual users we convince ourselves that we only enjoy certain things under the influence.

"Have you ever watched a sunset… on weed??"

As we gain more freedom from our addiction we are able to find more enjoyment in normal life. The sunset is still amazing, the music still sounds nice, the food still tastes good. It turns out we never needed marijuana to enjoy those things, we needed marijuana to satisfy our chemical cravings for THC. Without those cravings and artificially manipulated cycles of ups and downs, we are able to find joy and pleasure in each passing moment. In the hard moments, we are able to find opportunities for growth. In the boring moments, we are able to sit and think quietly, to get to know ourselves better.

We learn that we do not need constant stimulation. We do not need to be constantly looking for ways to escape from "real life". We learn to accept the present, and to recognize the parts we do not accept and make a plan to change them. We are able to honestly say-

"I am not running away from myself anymore."

Day 13

The topic of the day is Resistance. This concept comes to us from a wonderful book called The War of Art. In this book, author Stephen Pressfield discusses the idea of Resistance. He describes Resistance as the internal force that works against our self-improvement. Resistance is the force that tells us our creative ideas are silly or unrealistic. Resistance is what leads us to shelve our ideas and instead attempt to fill that creative void in easier ways.

Pick the book up, or get it on audio. It is a short read or listen, and it details concepts that are relevant to everyone. A main idea is that we all have some sort of driving impulse that is unique to us individually. Michael Jordan had to play basketball. Beethoven had to compose. Each of us has this sort of drive, this commission to do and create.

Resistance is the force that keeps us away from fulfilling these passions. We fall to distraction or demotivation or fear or despondency. We don't **do** what we are most wanting to do in life. This creates tension within us and it creates empty space and it creates bad feelings. People deal with this negative tension in all sorts of ways. They sleep all day. They drink. They cycle through dissapointing relationships. They jump off bridges. If you are reading all the way to day thirteen of this guide, there is a good chance your method of choice was marijuana.

Just like when we talked about denial, Resistance and marijuana go quite nicely together. We would create negative feedback loops, downward spirals for ourselves to be trapped in. The disassociative and spacey effects of marijuana make it hard to really tune into what your mind wants. Under the influence of marijuana, time becomes more abstract, the future doesn't make any sense. Ideas we have cycle from sounding amazing to sounding stupid in a matter of minutes. How can we map, direct and achieve growth from this state of mind?

We reach a place of frustration. "I have all these ideas but I can't get them off the ground. My life seems to be stuck." As we have discussed at length, what does the mind of the addict seek out for comfort and reward? We would get high and be temporarily satisfied, soothed and subdued. "What was all that fuss about? I feel fine. I feel better than fine, I feel nice and toasty and I could go for a snack."

Now that we are breaking free from this pattern, we are free to enter into new patterns. In fact, we have to or we will be dealing with the same problems forever, marijuana or not. But now, we are starting to gain clear head space.

(This is why the writing exercises are so helpful. Writing is a place between thought and action. We can write "I would like to start a carpet cleaning business" or "I am going to plan to go back to school", and this gets the thought out from bouncing around in our heads and causing tension, but it is a safe action without that consequences of just going out and buying a carpet cleaner or registering for classes. We can write out and develop these thoughts and they will naturally take shape over a period of time. The cream will rise to the top. We will be able to gain perspective on our own minds and see which ideas are our true wants and which we have just constructed.)

This clear head space gives us somewhere to work from. As we become more honest with ourselves and aware of the workings of our minds, we can make tremendous progress. The addicted mind can not really examine itself. It is not honest with itself. The addicted mind either says, "I am not addicted" or "I am addicted, but I don't care." Neither of these ideas are compatible with personal growth.

Now that we have said "I am addicted, and I do care, and I am breaking free" and we are doing the honest work to support that statement, we can grow.

Day 14

Two weeks! That is a milestone to be proud of. You are getting the hang of it. Now you have two weeks under your belt and you know that the first wasn't a fluke. You have turned your willpower into

action and you have started to internalize positive habits. You aren't out of the woods yet. Week 3 will be challenging in its own ways, but **you have the power to blast through it.**

You have more homework this week. I hope you did last week's.

Your first AA meeting can be an uncomfortable experience but I believe that it gives perspective and insight into the addicted mind. It is also a wonderful to see people coming together in community to fight back against their addictions. If you skipped it last week, I suggest attending this week. This week, your homework is to **give back.**

Find some sort of a volunteer opportunity or create your own. You have full flexibility. You can go pick up trash, wash dogs, chat with lonely elderly people, visit sick people, feed the homeless, whatever you like. The details are not important, what is important is the **action** and **intention** of giving back.

When we are so focused on self improvement and self help, it is good to take a step back and do something for others. It is important to get our own minds healed, but it is also important to maintain and foster a spirit of caring about and for other people. The addicted mind favors its own happiness over the happiness of other people. It is important that as we gain freedom from the addicted mind that we reset our brains in other ways, and spending time and energy focused on how we can help those around us is important. And you will feel good!

That is it for today. Give yourself a little treat in honor of two weeks free from pot. Think about where you want to volunteer. Take a nice long walk or sit in nature. Rub your feet. Get some exercise. **Keep doing your work**. You are well on your way into a difficult journey and you should be proud of yourself.

Day 15

In any situation, there are two places we can operate from- the position of weakness or the position of power. In relation to anything in the world, substance or circumstance, we are either the master or the mastered.

When you committed to breaking your addiction you immediately placed yourself in the position of power. Just the act of saying- "**I commit to changing this pattern**" puts you in charge. You are no longer being acted on, you are acting.

Now you are two weeks in, and you are gaining strength and momentum in that position of power. You are feeding off of your own strength and becoming stronger. Every day that you do not smoke is another day in your mental ammunition clip. Today you are over the hump in your 30 day journey. The other side is not easy either, but you have come a long way. I found that the other side of the hump was easier, and that after 30 days it continued to get easier. Our brains operate on short timelines. By now, you are well on your way to breaking the psychological ties marijuana was exercising on you. You are starting to operate from a position of strength.

In your using days, marijuana held the position of strength. You woke up and said,

"Maybe I won't smoke today"

and marijuana said, "Yeah right. Shut up and hit this."

And you did as you were told. The next day, you had even less motivation to stand up to your habit, even less faith in yourself and your ability to think freely. This is the position of weakness. It becomes a self-fulfilling prophecy. You think, "I can't escape this pattern" and then you prove yourself right.

Do you feel better now? Stronger? More empowered? I would hope so. You should! Every day you go without using is a big middle finger in the face to the habits that used to hold you hostage. As you get further stabilized into your position of strength you begin to find the idea of going back to your former ways as detestable. You become like someone who has escaped from jail. Why would you go back? You are running as fast as you can in the opposite direction, profoundly grateful for your freedom.

If you don't feel this way yet, don't worry. You are still breaking psychological ties. You are still adjusting to a new way of being. Your brain might feel confused or lost. You are in uncharted territory. Many people choose to stay in an uncomfortable and familiar place rather than risk the unknown. You have gone out into the uncomfortable unknown and you are figuring it out. You are using your position of power to further smash through psychological walls.

Every time you use a positive coping strategy, every time you shut down a craving, every time you turn down an opportunity to get high, you are further cementing in your mind the idea:

"I am powerful. I am free. I am the one who controls my actions and decides my habits. I will not be mastered by any substance."

Day 16

You have homework today. It might be uncomfortable. It will be productive.

You are far enough into your walk away from marijuana that we can start to look some more at the time you spent using. It is important to be looking forward, and to exist in the present, but it can be productive also to look at the past. We can't change the past. We shouldn't dwell there. But we can be honest about it and we can learn from it.

Your task today is to examine how your marijuana habit impacted the relationships you have with other people in your life. So far we have mainly been focusing on how our use impacted our relationship with ourselves. It is important to also pay attention to how we have affected others.

Are there people you care about who you have cut off or avoided because they disapproved of your use?

Have you checked out of important relationships because you were too stoned to focus?

Have your friendships with certain friends become based mostly on using marijuana together?

These are hard questions and the answers might not be clear. Maybe you were the type of user who could maintain present and productive relationships with all the people you cared about. I was not. I left a trail of relationship problems and a lot of them had to do with my various habits and substance misuses. If it came down to marijuana or a friendship, marijuana won.

The only real requirement of this exercise is that you be honest with yourself. We left denial in the past along with our other self-defeating habits.

If you feel compelled to apologize, do so. If you need to reach out, do that. If you feel that it is best to just leave certain relationships in the past, trust your instinct. Sometimes it is a helpful exercise to write a letter that you have no intention of sending. Sometimes it is enough to just sit and think.

Do no harm. Don't interfere in an old partner's healthy new relationship. Don't go by your old smoking buddies' house to talk if you know that will lead to you getting high together. Use your judgement and be careful with others and yourself.

It is important to remember that you are moving forward. You are now free from these old patterns. You don't have to make the same mistakes again. You can live as someone who knows where certain roads lead. Your journey has purpose. Positive change can come from examination of negative actions. Your justification comes from what you do from here forward. By choosing to move forward and not backwards you can heal yourself and others.

There is a verse in the Bible that says, "We know that in all things God works for the good of those who love Him, who have been called according to His purpose."

Regardless of your religious views, this is Truth for your life. You have been called for a purpose. You are on a journey to freedom because you care about what happens with your life. If you continue on the path of growth, all the actions of your past will be made useful.

Day 17

I was arrested for possession and part of my probation terms were that I attend "Substance Abuse Counseling." I thought the whole thing was a joke. Mostly it consisted of me paying $75 a session to watch 30 minute War on Drugs VHS tapes. I usually showed up stoned. At the end of 12 weeks, I poured my fake pee in the cup and passed my final drug test and I was given a certificate that proclaimed me "cured." I shook the therapist's hand, went out to my truck and fired up a blunt.

People don't stop using unless they want to stop using. The addicted mind will find all sorts of tips, tricks and loopholes. It will scheme and plot and lie in wait in order to obtain the fix that it wants.

Despite not taking any of it seriously, there was one video I found very interesting. It talked about "the addiction cycle."
The addiction cycle looks like this

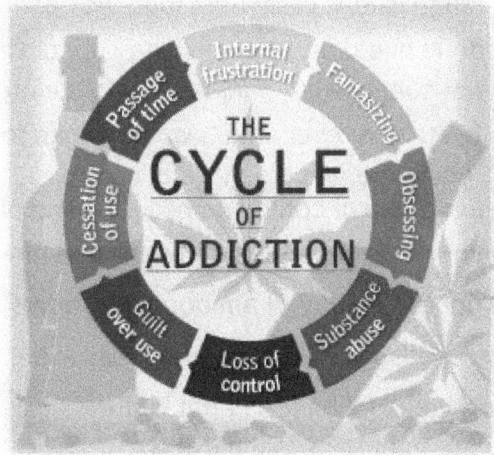

The cycle starts inside, independent of any substances. We have internal frustration and we seek to self medicate with whatever substance hits our own particular buttons.

From frustration, we go to fantasy. "If I could just get stoned I bet I would feel better."

After fantasy is obsession or fixation, "I bet Jim has some bud." "If I leave work right now I can get to the dispensary before it closes."

Have you ever made an excuse to go to a particular side of town or to leave a social engagement so you could get high? That is fixation. You have to get high.

After obsession, you do get high. Jim does have bud, or if he doesn't, John does. You convince your boss to let you out of work. Whatever you have to do, you do it. Then you stare at your bounty for a second, perform your using ritual, and get high.

Instant relief.

This relief turns to loss of control. We are lucky that with marijuana this stage is less prominent than with certain hard drugs or alcohol.

We don't overdose, we don't stay up for days or drive off the road.

Loss of control with marijuana looks different for different people, but if you have ever said "I won't smoke today" and then reneged on that, you experienced a loss of control.

After this loss of control comes a feeling of guilt. You are out of the position of power and into the position of weakness, and it doesn't feel good. You say, "I am done! No more!"

Time passes. You feel internal frustration. You think, "Man, I bet I would feel a lot better if I got high…."

You are right back in the cycle.

A lot of days I quit pot in the morning and was high as a kite by lunch.

The longer that we can learn to stay in the cessation period, the better our chances are of breaking free from the cycle. We have to learn to deal with the internal frustration in healthy ways and to shut down the fantasy before it becomes fixation.

As we get further away from the last time we used, the cycle has much less power. Instead of feeling guilt, we feel empowerment. As the chemical bonds break, we can see more clearly. We realize that feeling proud of ourselves feels a lot better than getting high ever did.

We chip away at that internal frustration and begin to convert it into internal peace and fulfillment.

We become fiercely protective of our own minds and our new place outside of the addiction cycle.

We accept that a single use will wipe out all of our progress and put us right back into the wheel.

We plan accordingly and keep **doing the work** of buying back our freedom.

Day 18

Today we are going a little further into the theoretical/psychological side of addiction.

We are going to talk about ritual.

Ritual is an important part of the addiction cycle. It is a physical tie to psychological feelings. On the addiction cycle we talked about yesterday, ritual falls right at the end of fixation. Our using ritual is the last thing we fixate on before we get high.

Think about how intently you used to roll joints. Or how carefully you would break your weed down and evenly distribute it into a bowl. Maybe every day you went to the same dispensary or on Mondays you caught a sale at one and had a different stop for Wednesday.

I know people who said they could not get all the way into vaping concentrates because they really liked the ritual of breaking down actual flower.

Smoking itself is filled with ritual. Marijuana is smoked in a circle with a defined rotation. There are code words and unwritten rules. You get the idea. (Even writing this just now I felt my mind drift to the very first stage of fantasy- fond remembrance. It is good not to dwell and it is important to shut such thoughts down immediately. If we let fantasy turn to fixation we are in for a tough battle.)

Any addictive behavior comes with a ritual. So not only do we have to break the patterns of use, we have to break our ties to the associated rituals. Time and distance are our friends here. The more space we put between ourselves and the old rituals that held us captive, the easier our job gets.

While you are early in your quit journey, don't go hang out at your old smoke spot. You will be tempted to fall into fantasy. As you get more days clean under your belt, these old ties will have less power over you. You will come to mostly forget your old rituals.

I think rituals have so much power because they let us turn our brains off. We do not have to think. We go on autopilot, and our brains know that there is a nice warm chemical bath at the end. This is an easy trap to fall into.

There is only so much space in the front of our brains. When one thing comes in to the foreground of our consciousness, it pushes something else into the back. As we live without marijuana, we are pushing those patterns and rituals further and further back and replacing them with new ones. Now you have rituals of growth. I wake up in the morning and make my bed. I like that ritual. It puts me in a mindset of achievement first thing, it reminds me that my actions lead to results.

Soon, the old rituals that held so much power over us will be distant memories. We will forget that marijuana even played a part. We will be excited about the new rituals and patterns and habits that we are cultivating.

We are no longer operating from a mindset of mindless repetition, we are operating from a mindset of growth and improvement.

Day 19

"They want you to be stoned."

This was the other major idea that I took away from my counseling sessions. The therapist had a bit of a conspiracy theorist bent and this was his statement about the proliferation of marijuana and alcohol and prescription drugs.

It is counterintuitive. We usually think about the government as a bunch of old fogies who want to ban weed and lock people up for using. I always had an idea that my using was some sort of act of rebellion against the "powers that be."

The reality was that the "powers that be" didn't care one way or another about my act of rebellion. They were happy to collect their fines and court costs. I got a small sense of smug satisfaction when I rolled past a cop and didn't get pulled over. I thought I was really getting one over on everybody.

I was really only fooling myself.

The 'powers that be' looove it when you pay more attention to getting high than to the corrupt actions they are taking. 'They want you to be stoned.' The more stuff that selfish people in power can get you hooked on, the happier they are. They are hoping that you will be too preoccupied to even notice them picking your pocket.

If you want to cause and create change, if you want to stand up to corrupt systems, it is best to come at it with a clear mind.

You can still fight the power. You can still be a counterculture hippie rebel if that is your thing. And you can do it with a clear mind and freedom from old habits. Anyone who tells you different is either trying to sell you something or uncomfortable with their own journey.

Breaking addictive ties is the ultimate rebellion. You are rebelling against the aspects of your own mind that would will to hold you back. You are rebelling against a substance that you once thought you loved.

If you get turned on by the idea of sticking it to the man, the best way to do it is to become self-realized and independently successful. If you do not deal with your own substance misuse patterns they will always hang over your head and hold you back. You are too smart for that. You are too aware. You are shaping your own destiny. Every day that you defend your brain against itself you make yourself stronger.

Day 20

You have probably noticed that certain places, smells, feelings and times bring up thoughts about using. We are creatures of habit. Our brains seek patterns and associations. The addicted brain wants to tie many of these patterns and associations back to the substance of choice. This goes along with the idea of ritual.

Sometimes we didn't even want to get high, we were just participating in our patterns of association. If I was going to the beach, or going fishing, I pretty much always got high beforehand. Why?

"Uh…. it's just what I do…."

If we were asking a beaver why it chewed on trees or a dog why it barked, that would be an alright answer. For us humans there are higher standards. We are responsible for examining and planning our actions. If we don't examine our actions we are doomed to drift through life without direction.

Why was that "just what I did?"

The root answer is association. My brain came to expect that certain actions and experiences would come with a marijuana high. We have talked already about the drug of choice being the ultimate reward in the addicted person's brain. Going to the beach or going fishing were irrelevant. What my brain was excited about was the accompanying high. If there was no weed, the experience felt tainted or not as good. I would be fantasizing about getting high or trying to figure out how I could get high.

The sad truth of how this often plays out is that we bail out on meaningful social experiences because they would cut into our pot smoking. We don't want to go visit family because we will either have to avoid smoking or figure out some way to sneak tokes. We reconsider taking certain trips because it might be hard to get high, or we spend the first day of our vacation trying to track down a sack in a new location.

All of this distracts from enjoyment of the present moment. When we think, "This is ok, but I could be getting high right now instead", we are not really living life. We are existing in some fantasy. Our relationships and our quality of life suffer as a result.

As we walk away from marijuana, it can be tempting to reminisce. Our brains want us to remember the fun times, the good times, the easy times.
Don't fall for it.

When you are tempted to think about some good time you had getting high, remember all the negative stuff that came as a direct result of your unhealthy relationship with marijuana. And remember that as you repair your brain, these associations will be less powerful. Guess what, I still enjoy going to the beach. I like it even more now. I can be **at** the beach, instead of thinking about walking back to the car to roll up again every hour or two. As your mind is repaired you find joy and meaning in the same things you always did, but your experiences are not hazed out. You build new associations of enjoyment that are not drug related.

It is a great feeling to be happy and content to just sit in the sun, with a quiet and clear mind.

Day 21

Congratulations! You have made it three weeks! It is a common theory that when we do something 21 days in a row it will become a habit. If this is true, you are now in the habit of **not** smoking pot. This is something to be proud of. I found that by 21 days in I was feeling good and had a much stronger feeling of conviction than even a week before. There will always be work and maintenance, but you are well on your way to freedom. You are three weeks into a power position. **Keep going.**

You have new homework this week, but this time it's fun homework. This week, you will answer the question:

"What else can I accomplish?"

21 days ago, 21 days without marijuana probably seemed daunting if not impossible. And yet here we are. What else seems daunting and impossible? Think you can get there too? I think you can. You know you can.

We have talked a lot about the position of power. We are going to talk about it some more, because I think it's really important. Right now you have momentum on your side. You made a big promise to yourself and kept it and now you are feeling strong and proud and motivated. You are in a position of strength. Use that position! Set yourself up to stay in that position of power, to seek out and achieve new accomplishments.

Now that you are not using you have more time, more money and more clarity. That is a recipe for action. Three weeks ago, you had a limiting idea in your mind, the idea that you needed to use marijuana. Now you have proven that limiting idea wrong. What other limiting beliefs do you have and how can you break through them?

An exercise I have found to be helpful relies on the two column system also. On one side, write small/realistic ideas and goals. Things that you could probably accomplish with your current resources and knowledge, or at least see a possibility to accomplish. On the other side write huge, wild goals. The kind that seem unattainable, impossible.

This exercise helps to open the mind to the idea of endless possibilities. Are those goals really unattainable, or are you just thinking through a self-limiting mindset? If they are out of reach for now, you have a list of more tangible goals that you can take action steps toward. You are getting those wild ideas out of your head and onto paper, where you have a chance to focus and refine them. Maybe there is overlap between your regular goals and your huge goals. Maybe thinking about your dream goals will help you to better steer your shorter-term goals. Maybe you will see steps that you can take in the short term to help realize your big goals down the line.

You are actively destroying a major self-limiting thought and behavior pattern and replacing it with positive patterns. This is huge. Every day you make yourself stronger. You uphold your convictions and feel proud of yourself. These feelings of strength in yourself are therapeutic and they set you up for action and success in other areas of your life as well.

Keep doing the work.

Day 22

Did you get a chance to read or listen to War of Art? If not, I still recommend it. Today we are going to talk about Resistance some more. There is an important concept in the War of Art about Resistance sometimes being strongest at the end. A writer gets to the last chapter of a book and then deletes the whole thing. We get close to where we want to be and then we lower our guard. Resistance sees our weakness and pounces on it.

Don't let that happen. You have come too far and you are doing too well. Our goal is to continue to grow and improve. We are working to fully subdue the part of our brain that used to drive us to abuse marijuana. When that part of our brain says "I bet you can smoke just this once and be fine" or " Remember how much fun we used to have" or "What's the point of all this anyway? You know you'll screw up again", we stick our fingers in both our ears and go "LALALALALALALA CAN'T HEAR YOU."

We are moving forward. We expect Resistance, we plan for it, and we shut it down immediately. We don't give it any chance to make a home in our minds. The quicker and more firmly we put a stop to Resistance, the less power it holds.

As we learn to identify Resistance and call it out we become more skilled at dealing with it and overcoming it. As we learn about the forces that work on our brains we can recognize them and become more aware. As we are more aware we can be more honest.

Expect Resistance as it relates to staying away from marijuana. There will be temptation and your brain will try to trick you. Expect Resistance elsewhere. A major part of this whole plan involves figuring out what drives you, what excites you, where you want to go and what you want to do. Resistance will try to lead you away from those things. As we get less chemically and psychologically tied to marijuana, we find that it was not the cause of all our problems.

Some days we still want to sleep in. We don't feel like doing the dishes. We can't get our minds out of the fog. Our creative endeavors hit roadblocks.

The way to defeat Resistance is to choose to **do your work.** If you have a regular job, you have to show up even on days when you don't feel like it. Sometimes it is raining, sometimes there is traffic, sometimes you have a headache. You still have to go. That is how we should treat our personal work, the work that we feel inspired and instructed to do. We should take this personal work even more seriously, should guard it even more jealously against forces that try to steal our attention for it.

I assume you have heard people say, "Find a job you love and you'll never work a day in your life." This is equal parts truth and bullshit. This does not just apply to jobs in the traditional sense, but to any act of creation or production that we undertake. It is true that when you do what you love and are passionate about you will feel a deep sense of satisfaction, better than any high you used to get or amusement you can take part in. It is bullshit that you will not work. You will get up early, you will stay up late. You will sweat and pace and sometimes get so fed up you have to walk away. You will put in many hours that no one sees or offers thanks for. **You will work.** Work is good. Work is your friend. Work is how we defeat Resistance and get to where we want to be.

Day 23

"If you fail to plan, you can plan to fail."

Sometimes great things come from winging it. Spontaneity is fun and it is important to keep your mind open to all possibilities. More often, great ideas become reality as the result of a plan. Our minds get cluttered and distracted. We see something shiny or hear the wind blow and we are lost. It is very helpful when we have a plan that we can return to.

I have long been an anti-planner. It makes me uncomfortable to agree to anything more than about 20 minutes in advance. There are so many possibilities in any situation that I have a hard time limiting myself to just one. This leads to the **paradox of choice.** When you are at the grocery store and you go to the ketchup aisle, there are 15 different kinds of ketchup. You stand there and stare at them for five minutes, trying to figure out which one is the best. That is wasted time. The same thing applies to our lives. This is where planning has helped me immensely.

A well thought out plan helps us to eliminate options that are not interesting or productive to us. It saves time and energy. A brief planning period leads to much more focused and efficient work. Plans work on large scales and small scales. We can plan our day, and we can plan our life. Plans change. Things come up, our focus shifts, we get different or better ideas along the way. A plan is there to provide a framework and a guide that we can place the smaller details into.

I knew that I wanted to write this guide and I sat down to do it. I blew through Day 1 and then stared at a blank Day 2 screen for a long time. Eventually I had the idea to write down a list of topics I wanted to cover, laid them out by day and started knocking them out one at a time. It made the task immensely easier. A plan is a way to break down a large task into more manageable pieces. Think about your quit journey. When we try to say "I will never smoke pot again for the rest of my life no matter what", we get overwhelmed and then frustrated and most of the time we relapse. When we take it one day at a time while also trying to figure out the bigger picture, we have a lot more success.

By eliminating marijuana and/or other substances that we were dependent on we give ourselves a clear platform to operate from. Think of it like sweeping out a room. Hopefully this clarity of mind combined with some of the exercises from this course have helped you to get a better idea about what some of the big picture things you care about are. Think about what you really want to achieve, feel, give and do. Write it down. Keep writing it down until it is a clear one or two sentence idea.

This one or two sentence idea is where your plan starts. You can fill in as many or as few blanks as you want. You can make lists, draw diagrams, create schedules and timelines. There is lots of room for flexibility. Your plan is not a prophecy or statement of fact, it is something that you can look at when you feel lost. It is a way for you to keep your eye on the large scale idea of what you want while creating action steps for all of the pieces that lead there.

Your plan will help you define your purpose and it will work in conjunction with it.

Day 24

There is an old Calvin and Hobbes cartoon that shows Calvin screaming "Happiness isn't good enough for me! I demand euphoria!"

It is meant to be funny, but isn't that how we used to live? This lifestyle worked against us. As we constantly chased euphoria it became difficult to experience happiness. Happiness is sustainable. When we figure out our own personal path to happiness we can move in that direction daily without too much effort. Euphoria requires constant input and effort. You know this. Our marijuana use led to a routine of getting high and then trying to get higher. When I felt the comedown, it was time to fire up another one. Repeat until bedtime, start again tomorrow.

The purpose of this whole process is to flip Calvin's statement.

"Euphoria isn't good enough for me! I demand happiness!"

We had to put aside our quest for euphoria in order to get back on track toward happiness. We eventually figured out that euphoria was lying to us also. Chemically induced nice feelings a few times a day stopped being enough to satisfy us. We had to reset our brains. This meant stopping the artificial ups and downs so we could relearn how to be **happy** without external input.

Why were you chasing euphoria?

This is a complex question with many answers, but spend a little time thinking about it. Eventually it became a matter of trying to scratch a chemical itch, but try to think before or outside of that. What was it that appealed to you? **What were you running from?** You are powering through chemical ties of your addiction and you are breaking loose of the psychological bonds, but it is important to deal with the roots. When you pull a weed it will grow back if you don't get the root.

For a lot of us, myself included, much of this chasing after euphoria came from a desire to kill time. I knew I was not exercising my potential and that made me uncomfortable. When I got high, I was comfortable and I was not really thinking about the time I was wasting anymore. I was euphoric because I could not bring myself to do the work of finding happiness. I did not want to look for happiness because it seemed like too much work. I did not want to do work because it was easier in the short term to seek out euphoria.

Your experience may be the same or it may be different. The details are part of your own personal journey. What matters is that you can recognize them and be honest about them. "The Truth will set you free." This applies in the case of dealing with yourself just as much as it applies to relations with others.

Day 25

Remember Rip Van Winkle? He fell asleep in the woods and woke up a hundred years later. As you come back into life without a marijuana habit you may feel a bit like Rip.

"What did I miss?", you think, rubbing your eyes.

Like we have already talked about, it is not good to dwell but it is good to be aware. As you are further away from your last use you can examine yourself a little more critically without risking a relapse. Spend a little time thinking about what you might have missed during your time spent using habitually. The point is not to feel guilty or sorry for yourself, it is to make yourself aware of the hidden costs associated with the habit. This can be a powerful tool when you are tempted moving forward. Another helpful aspect of this exercise is that it gives you an idea of where to aim moving forward.

If you feel like you missed out on educational opportunities because you were busy smoking weed, now is a great time to figure out how to get started on them now. If you feel like you missed out on building real friendships and connections, that is something you can pay attention to from today forward. Whatever you feel that you missed, it is not too late to find it. The best time to plant a tree was ten years ago. The second best time is today.

Being aware of these feelings of loss is important. If we are aware, we will be conscious. We can figure out ways to incorporate these desires into our Big Picture Plan and our daily habits. We can narrow them down and examine where they come from.

It seems a common thread among former heavy users that heavy use goes hand in hand with lack of social growth. This is maybe not your experience, but it was mine. I was way more interested in smoking a blunt on my couch by myself or with my using buddies than I was in putting myself out there to make new friends or attend some type of event. I used marijuana as a social shield. It was an easy way to instantly screen out relationships with lots of people. If my habit made someone uncomfortable, that made me uncomfortable, and so it was much easier to just isolate and avoid.

Another common thread is the idea of professional or educational stagnation. Maybe you had even managed to be "successful" while you had your habit. I believe there is a good chance that on some level you wished you were achieving more, or achieving in a different direction. Marijuana helped us to quiet our discomfort and justify our inaction.

This is not your reality anymore! **You are free!** You can be who you want and do what you want. You have shooed away the cloud that hung over your head. You are opening your mind and narrowing your focus and planning out action steps. My hope for this guide is that it helps you break free of the immediate chains of a marijuana habit. But I don't want to see you wandering around, loitering outside the jail waiting for something to do. I want you to realize that you have a **purpose**, and you already know what it is. You knew the whole time. It was scary to deal with and we tried to hide it in different ways, but it burned under the surface the whole time. Now you are setting it free and putting in the **work** to turn your dreams and goals into reality.

Day 26

A few years ago a man I worked with was telling me about his recent divorce from an unhappy and mentally abusive relationship. He was aware that the relationship was unhealthy, but in some ways he still missed it. He used this metaphor,

"If you carry a stone in your pocket for a year and you take it out, you will notice that it's gone."

We can expect to have some of this same mental reaction in terms of our former marijuana habit. There are bound to be good memories mixed in, fond remembrances. A long period of habitual use means you may have years of memories that prominently feature marijuana. You don't have to block these memories, but if you want to progress you have to leave them in the past.

The burden of a habitual dependency is that it doesn't allow for casual use. You can't go back to how it was and truthfully you don't want to. The more aware parts of your nature are glad to have freedom and clarity. Operate from that place of awareness instead of being swayed by feeling. Remember the addiction cycle. If you spend very much time reminiscing it will quickly turn into fantasy. Once we get invested in the fantasy stage it can be hard to stop the cycle. If we let fantasy turn to fixation it is extremely hard. The fixated addict will jump through a lot of hoops in order to obtain a fix. We have to continue to guard our minds against temptation and fantasy.

Your life was not all sunshine and rainbows when you were smoking pot. It is good to be free. Remember both of these truths and be quick to come back to them when you are tempted.

If you check your exes' Facebook page fifteen times a day, are you really over them? You don't want to be awkwardly avoiding marijuana, you want to be **free** from marijuana. The less time you spend fondly remembering your old habits, the quicker that freedom will come.

You are going to develop new memories. As you remove more and more limitations from your mind you will be able to experience all kinds of exciting things. You will be fully present and you will be able to remember them better later.

Life is trippy enough without weed. You will still have plenty of fun. As marijuana gets further in your past, smaller in your rearview mirror, forgetting about it will be easier. Keep moving forward, one day at a time.

Day 27

What should you do about your friends who still use?

The answer to that will be complex and differ greatly based on your individual situation.
The short answer:

Love them, encourage them, accept that you may be on different journeys.

If you have a friend who respects your decision to quit and doesn't pressure you to get high with them then by all means continue your friendship with that person. If you are in a position to get high and you willfully turn it down you strengthen your convictions and increase your feelings of self respect. Your friend might even notice a change in you and consider reevaluating their own habits. It is not our place to speak on other people's lives and decisions. We can share our own experiences and feelings, but our friends do not want to hear a sermon from us.

If your friend tries to pressure you into smoking or question your conviction, it is good to spend more time away from the situation. Your friend is probably not being malicious. When people are uncomfortable with themselves or their situation, sometimes their reaction is to project that onto others. You have made a powerful and difficult change in your life and some people will react to that with jealousy. A friend who backlashes your decision to refrain from marijuana is probably partially sad to lose you as a smoking buddy and also dealing with internal turmoil about their own habit. They might wish they could quit, or even subconsciously **know** that they should quit but not be ready to come to terms with that knowledge. Encourage them! Gently remind them that you are no different than them, and that a month ago you also thought freedom was impossible. Tell them honestly about some of the benefits you are experiencing. And then leave it alone. People will come to things when they are ready and pushiness will only breed resentment. A friend who is comfortable in their own habits and state will probably not hassle you about what you are doing.

Sometimes, the fact is that we just outgrow friendships. We can still care about these people and even keep in occasional touch, but it is good to be selfish about our own growth. We can be generous with many other things, but our own mental health and growth should be closely guarded. You will find that new friends who are more aligned with your new path will show up and fill in some blank spots.

You will find that friendship with your own mind is the best kind of friendship there is. People move in and out of our lives. People are wonderful and it is good and healthy and fun to share life with them. You are stuck with your brain for life. You can move across the country or the world, quit your job, get in shape, get out of shape, use all sorts of substances: your mind stays with you. If you are not comfortable sitting alone with yourself, satisfied to look in the mirror at yourself, your problems will follow you wherever you go. When you deal with your mind, as we have been doing, you will have peace wherever you go. You will become unattached to places and circumstance as you build a fortress in your mind. You will be able to truthfully say that you are your own best friend.

Day 28

28 Days Later. Does it feel good to no longer be a zombie? Remember trying to get your eyes to open all the way? Having to read something 5 times because you kept forgetting the beginning of the sentence by the time you got to the middle?

You should be proud of yourself. Four weeks is a long time. You have broken the physical ties of marijuana. The psychological bonds are exponentially weaker than they were a month ago. You are in a position of power in your life, exercising agency. You can feel a sense of accomplishment and pride in yourself.

Today, I want you to make a decision. It will be a tough one. Maybe you already did it. I want you to decide whether you are going to keep your paraphernalia or get rid of it. And if you decide to get rid of it, I want you to do so. Make a little ceremony out of it if you'd like. The pipes etc. that you used to smoke with carry attachments and associations. It is mentally freeing to have them gone.

An old man that used to mentor me would always tell the story about when him and his wife quit using (pot and otherwise) some 30 or 40 years ago. He said he "walked out back and threw all the dope bags in the lake." This always stuck with me. The action of throwing away drugs and drug related items can help further cement change in our brain. It is a physical representation of the mental act of letting go.

You are saying, "I want this stuff out of my house and out of my life," and then you are acting on that thought. I can't tell you not to give away or sell expensive/sentimental pieces but I urge you to consider smashing them on the concrete instead. There is a mental release that comes with that action. You are telling yourself, "I **really** don't care about this stuff anymore, I just want to get rid of it and put it even further in the past."

If you are not ready to get rid of your paraphernalia, that is ok too. It can take a long time to fully let go of all attachments. Lock it up and continue to put in the work one day at a time. When you are ready you will get rid of the remainders.

The more we internalize a distancing from marijuana, the better our chances for long term success. Whether or not you smash your bong isn't really the important part. The important part is whether or not you smash your mental constraints and dependencies. Four weeks willingly staying free from pot is a great set up to much longer term success. You have the momentum, you are building the habits, you are putting space between your present life and your old associations.

Keep doing the work. If you let your mind wander, it will. If you indulge fantasies of getting stoned, you will eventually fulfill them. **If you hang out at the barbershop, you're gonna get a haircut.**

Take pride in what you have accomplished and be prepared to accomplish even more.

Day 29

Bad news today. Ready?

Quitting marijuana is not a way to magically teleport to where you want to be in life.

For someone who has a marijuana dependence, quitting will probably be the most important factor and first step to getting there. It is the issue that needs to be dealt with before all the others because it plays a part in all others. There will be times when you feel like you're not where you need to be. Sometimes you will not be the version of yourself that you want to be.

You might be tempted to think, "What's the point? I'm the same as before but now I can't get high."

This line of thought is a lie and you should not believe. When we were dependent on marijuana we couldn't even participate in honest self-evaluation. Any attempt at change or introspection was directly influenced by how stoned we were at that current moment. Marijuana dependency is a constant cycle of ups and downs, highs and lows. When we are high, we can examine ourselves, find things we want to work on, and start the process. When we are low, all that goes out the window because our number one priority is getting back to high.

Now that we have broken out of that cycle, we can get back on the path to **real** growth. The progress we make is honest. We are learning to recognize and handle our emotional changes in a healthy manner. Learning to manage our own minds is enough work for a whole lifetime. We should be proud and grateful for any progress we make.

We all have non-productive or destructive habits. It is sometimes easy to blame these habits on external forces. "I am lazy because I smoke pot." This is not the full story. Pot does make laziness feel extra nice and make it harder to get motivated. But we can still be lazy without any chemical help. It is an **internal** battle, the same way that escaping our marijuana dependency was an internal battle.

Rest assured that whatever your vices and hangups are, you are not alone. Nobody is perfect, not even people who have recently stopped smoking weed. You are on a journey. Some days you will walk on a nice flat road and some days you will have to struggle up a hill. Both days, you are moving forward. That is the important part.

If you put the work in, you will change the habits and patterns you wish to change. You will see improvement where you work towards improvement. Use this past month as a reference point. Do you feel different today than you did a month ago? It is because you made a commitment and **put the work in.** That process can be repeated over and over again with the same results.

When we take responsibility of our own lives and act with power, positive change results.

Day 30
You made it! Congratulations!

You have made it through 30 days without marijuana.

Don't let yourself or anyone else trivialize that accomplishment. The actual abstinence from pot is important, but what is really important is that you have proven to yourself that you have the ability to direct your own reality. You can deal with the ups and downs of life without chemical help. When you make a commitment to yourself and trust yourself to keep it. We used to try to redirect our reality in unhealthy ways by getting stoned and trying to escape from it. Now that we are living in reality instead of running from it we are able to shape it.

What comes next?

It is up to you!

You can do whatever you want. Hell, you can spark up a big fat joint and go right back to your old life if you want. I hope that is not what you want. I hope you want to keep rocketing forward. Now that you have established a baseline of freedom from marijuana dependency you are able to reach the next level of progress. Your next 30 days will be easier and you will see larger scale progress.

Spend some more time on your Big Picture Plan and your daily habits list. Tune them both up. Experiment. See what works and what doesn't, what you like and what you don't. Write things down. Get up early. Exercise.

Create.

Creation is rebellion against the darkness. Creation is a physical representation of the best parts of our souls. The medium you create in is not important. You know what you want to do, what you need to do. Do it.

Creation will breed more creation. Momentum is natural and unstoppable. When you are bouncing all over the place you slow down your momentum. When you are living in negative patterns you have negative momentum. When you set your eyes forward and move towards that, even an inch at a time, you are building momentum.

I don't have anything else to say. Thank you for reading this far. I hope you have found this guide to be helpful. I hope you have found freedom from habits that were not serving you. I hope you will continue to have success in your endeavors. I hope you will continue to grow in your freedom.

Be blessed.

www.ingramcontent.com/pod-product-compliance
Lightning Source LLC
Chambersburg PA
CBHW031614040426
42452CB00006B/519